# HOW CAN GOD
# ALLOW SUCH THINGS?

# HOW CAN GOD
# ALLOW SUCH THINGS?

.........................................

*by Dr. Richard Steinpach*

GRAIL·FOUNDATION·PRESS

GAMBIER, OHIO

2nd edition

Cataloging-in-Publication Data
155.2
STE
Steinpach, Richard, 1917-1992
How Can God Allow Such Things? : manuscript of a lecture by Richard Steinpach.–
Gambier, OH : Grail Foundation Press, ©1995.
96 p. ; 23 cm.
Includes bibliographies.
Summary: Applies the basic laws of nature to our life on earth and our life in the
beyond.
ISBN 1-57461-009-0 (pbk.)
1. Reincarnation  2. Adjustment (Psychology)
155.2
613.2—dc20

*Cover Art: LM Design*
*Typesetting: LM Design*
*Printer: Malloy Lithographing, Inc.*

*Printed on recycled paper.*

*Books by Dr. Richard Steinpach*


BIRTH AND JUSTICE
FALSE WAYS
HOW CAN GOD ALLOW SUCH THINGS
IT HAS BEEN DEMONSTRATED
THE LECTURES
"SEE THE TRUTH IS SO NEAR AT HAND..."
SELF-KNOWLEDGE
THE WAY AND THE GOAL
WHAT GOETHE WISHED TO TELL US
WHY WE LIVE AFTER DEATH

"If there is a meaning in life at all, there must be a meaning in suffering."

–*Viktor E. Frankl*
*"Man's Search for Meaning"*

*This book contains the translation according to
the sense of the original German text.
In some cases the words of the translation can
only render the original meaning approximately.
Nevertheless, the reader will come to a
good understanding if he or she absorbs inwardly
the meaning of the contents.*

❦

.....................................................

**W**here, in any particular instance, we are unable to perceive the correlation between cause and effect...it merely proves the inadequacy of our ability to judge, but by no means the absence of justice!

.....................................................

# C O N T E N T S

..........................................................

..........................................................

. . . . . . . . . . . . . . . . . . . . . . . . . . . . . . . . . . . . . . .

*B*etween 1979 and 1990, Richard
Steinpach gave hundreds of lectures on
various topics all over the German-
speaking world. The powerful response
to his lectures not only confirmed the
relevance of the topics he discussed, but also compelled him
to publish them in book form. Grail Foundation Press is
pleased to publish Dr. Steinpach's works in America for
the first time.

. . . . . . . . . . . . . . . . . . . . . . . . . . . . . . . . . . . . . . .

*M*any of the world's most distinguished scientists, philosophers, educators and religious and political leaders convened in San Francisco, California during September, 1995 at the **State of the World Forum**, a multi-year, global initiative sponsored by the Gorbachev Foundation. Their mission was to articulate the fundamental priorities, values and actions necessary to constructively shape our common future. They addressed the statement by Václav Havel,

> "There are good reasons for suggesting that the modern age has ended. Many things indicate that we are going through a transitional period, when it seems that something is on the way out and something else is painfully being born. It is as if something were crumbling, decaying, and exhausting itself while something else still indistinct were arising from the rubble."

The **State of the World Forum** sought to address such questions as global anarchy, and the roots of human violence, social and economic liberty versus license, the drug crisis, the reformation of science and technology and the search for Divinity in the midst of chaos. Many came seeking answers to these questions in their personal lives.

Everyone, from the highest political leader to the simplest man on the street acknowledges the progressive and *distressing chaos and suffering in our world. Everywhere one looks one finds discord, disease, destruction and degeneration in the environment, our institutions, our individual lives as well as in our relationships and the greater society. We fear for our children and for the future. How did we get into this crisis situation? How are we to extricate ourselves from it?*

*Political summits are held, religious conferences convene, innumerable books are written...and the persistent questions "why" and "how" remain unanswered. As one of the three hundred and fifty participants in this historic event, I listened to each speaker and could only think to myself, "I wish every member of this forum would read **this** book!" For fundamentally, Steinpach has succeeded in exposing "how" and "why" the world is in its present state.*

*What, in fact, do people really mean when they say "How can God allow such things?" Perhaps when uttered angrily in a moment of desperation, it is a declaration of blame. Can we blame God for the particular circumstances and experiences of our lives? Expressed as a plea for help it, at the very least, reveals our confusion in the midst of disaster.*

*Many turn away from religion because they perceive a serious incongruity between their religious beliefs and the reality of their daily experiences. Science, in an explosion of new discoveries of unprecedented scope presents an evolving view of the cosmos that challenges our previously held ideas concerning God, creation and man. Through this view we can begin to observe an order and exactness in the micro-*

*cosmic and macrocosmic manifestations of life that is mind-boggling in its complexity and yet awe inspiring in its uniformity, perfection and simplicity.*

*Where does man's free will fit in this intricate picture? Where does his responsibility begin? As the creature with the most highly developed intellect, whose influence on the material world is so painfully visible, are we the masters of the universe as science leads us to believe? If so, how can we reconcile that notion with a religious belief that seeks to relinquish responsibility to a capricious, inscrutable or elusive God? Do we intuitively sense that each experience, whether painful or pleasant, is meant to serve a deeper purpose than we are willing to recognize?*

*Perhaps more importantly, the question "How can God allow such things?" brings to light our desire to understand how and why misfortune strikes. The wanting to understand the "how's" and "why's" of our misfortunes catapults us into our personal and collective mission as human beings. If we are not to abdicate all responsibility to an unfathomable God, who then is responsible?*

*In this book, Dr. Richard Steinpach leads us to an appreciation of the unity of the spiritual and material world, and man's pivotal role within it as an intelligent and responsible creature. By applying the basic Laws of Nature, Richard Steinpach has successfully brought together two worlds that have remained separated until now: the physical material world and the ethereal world of the spirit. If people truly understood how the Natural Laws, as explained by Steinpach, underpin everything spiritual and material, they would dramatically change how they live. With Steinpach's insight, we need never again cry despairingly, "How can God allow such things?", for the real question is, "How can man allow such things?"*

*As the architects of our own destiny, we can determine for ourselves—must determine for ourselves, in fact—whether or not we will use this brief time granted us on earth, to paraphrase Havel, in order to "crumble and decay, or to arise from the rubble." Dr. Steinpach shows how we are responsible not only to ourselves but also to a Higher Order in creation. Acknowledging this all-encompassing and awe-inspiring impartiality and perfection must bring every serious observer to a genuine recognition of God.*

Ifeoma Ikenze, MD
San Rafael, California

# HOW CAN GOD
# ALLOW SUCH THINGS?

*Manuscript of*
*a lecture by*
*Dr. Richard Steinpach*

*I*n recent years I have given a lecture in many cities entitled *"Why We Live After Death."* In the course of this lecture I mentioned the concept of fate. One evening at the conclusion of my explanations, an obviously-upset young man approached me, saying, "You speak of fate! Then what can you tell this girl?" He pointed to a young, beautiful woman in a wheelchair, perhaps paraplegic, the victim of an accident.

Well, what is there really to say in such a case? A few hackneyed phrases won't settle it. The question calls for careful consideration of so-called inscrutable relationships. Indeed, it is not an isolated question. Every day thousands pose this question in a similar way, for behind it lies man's primitive fear of being at the mercy of pure chance, of an inexplicable arbitrariness, which at the intervention of some fateful event in our lives, repeatedly gives rise to the question: "Why just him, her, or me?"

It extends also beyond the personal. Why do catastrophes sometimes strike groups of people; why must entire peoples suffer starvation and distress, physical or spiritual bondage? Again and again the question forces itself upon us: "Why?"

And ultimately it leads to the critical question: "If He, *God,* exists at all, how can He, of Whom it is said that He is loving and just, how can He permit all this?"

Can an answer really be found to this question in view of all the terrible things that happen in this world every single day? That I nonetheless propose to supply an answer is simply because some thirty years ago I had the good fortune to come to know the book, *In the Light of Truth: The Grail Message,* by Abd-ru-shin. This work contains the answer to this and to all our questions, for it explains our existence within the entire structure of Creation. Consequently, events take on a totally different dimension from the way we are accustomed to viewing them.

Knowing this work, I was greatly shocked when, in Austria, a well-known representative of a large religious community, asked by a reporter for his reaction to the famines, the massacres, and the plight of refugees, replied, "At such times I sometimes doubt the Justice of God."

Well, when even those who ought to give us clarity and hope suffer from doubt, when even they stand confounded before the events of our time, then something must have gone wrong. Have we been given a false picture of *God*, to Whom Love and Justice are therefore alien? Are our conceptions of these mistaken?

This is indeed the case, for what do we know of Justice? What do we know of Love? If these two concepts are to be used as a measure of Divinity, should they not be elevated in our thoughts beyond all possibility of doubt?

We regard it as just when good is rewarded and evil is punished. But we expect the relationship between cause and effect to be discernible to us. Where the connection is lacking, an occurrence appears to be unjust. It cannot be classified; it stands alone and thus has no intelligible meaning.

And what about our idea of love? To us love, to the degree that it is actually free of self-seeking, means doing good to others. But here we already stumble into new questions, for what is good? On this alone opinions certainly differ widely.

Just two sentences from the aforementioned work, however, indicate why we ask these questions. There we read:

4

*"Divine Love weaves... only what benefits every human spirit, but not what pleases and seems agreeable to it on earth. Divine Love goes far beyond this, because it governs the whole of existence."*

Now you see: it is first of all the human spirit to which reference is made. But what is generally known about the spirit? What is known of what benefits this spirit and of the entirety of our existence? Are you quite clear about it? If you express uncertainty about the answer to this question, then you have the reason for our misguided way of thinking, for in this uncertainty lies the root of our failure to understand.

Spirit continues to be something utterly vague to many; we confuse it with our reasoning power, even doubting its very existence. Yet spirit, and only spirit, is the actual essence of every human being, the only living thing within us. The physical body is merely the covering for this spirit. This covering is adapted to the nature of this world, enabling it to live and work here. But whatever happens in our existence concerns this *spirit*, proceeds from it, and relates to it.

In order to judge what benefits the spirit, we would have to know the meaning of our existence, for to benefit means simply to serve a purpose, to attain to some goal. For the human spirit this goal lies in its development, in gaining an ever greater understanding of the Laws of Creation. At the same time this also means gaining an increasing awareness of the potentialities contained within itself. For this, experience is required, which due to the nature of the human

5

spirit, can only be had initially in this dense-material earthly world. Like any meaningful education it must begin from the ground up. The well-known behavioral physiologist Konrad Lorenz has expressed it very aptly. We are, he says, "the missing link between ape and man." We have developed our human abilities, that is to say, those of the spirit, only to the smallest degree. Hence we are only "beings in the process of development." Why this is so and for what reason we could not be created perfectly immediately is explained to us in *The Grail Message*, but it would be going too far to deal with it here. However, this becomes evident: when *The Grail Message* teaches that we have within us "spirit germs" in need of development, this coincides with scientific understanding.

Yet instead of at last realizing the fact that we are here in order to learn from experiences, to make up for what has been neglected and to go on learning, we think that we are here to lead an agreeable life. Anything that is not consistent with this idea we deem as irreconcilable with Divine Love, for this Love, so we believe, must ensure us this agreeable life.

This present earth-life, however, is but a tiny segment within the whole of our existence. And it is only to that whole that everything is directed. When we complete the "training" we can return to our spiritual home. There, having become knowing and forever removed from transient material substance, we can joyfully and eternally cooperate in the working of Creation.

Ignorance about the true purpose of our existence, however, is the root of all evil. It does not even allow us to contemplate relationships whose starting point lies beyond our present range of vision. Let us become aware of this absurdity: knowing neither what came before nor what is to follow, we yet obstinately insist that the relationship between cause and effect be made manifest to us in the immediate tininess of our present life span, if we are to view it as just.

That is why *The Grail Message* tells us:

"*But one of the principal mistakes so many people make is that they only... take into consideration one earth-life, whereas in reality they already have several earth-lives behind them. These, as well as the intervening times in the Ethereal World, are equal to one uniform existence through which the threads are tightly stretched, without breaking, so that in the effects of a particular earthly existence only a small part of these threads therefore becomes visible.*"

Rebirth is a necessity in our process of development, which like the succession of classes at school, serves as further education or the opportunity to make up for things we have not understood. The knowledge about it is very old. To much of humanity it is the basis of their religious conceptions. As we can gather from the New Testament, it was also common knowledge when Jesus lived on earth. In other lectures I have already explained what led, in the year 553, to the disappearance of references to repeated earth-lives in the Christian religion. Because of the significance of this event I must briefly reiterate that it was a purely political dictate by the Roman Emperor Justinian.

To him the relatively young and subordinate Church had to defer. Subsequently, the Church could and can no longer remedy that situation without losing its credibility.

The loss of this knowledge, however, was a monstrosity perpetrated against Western peoples. They were spiritually caged—worse still, immured. Their conception of life was reduced to this one earthly existence. Instead of seeing joyfully before them the broad span of the spirit's path of development, Western men and women came to view death as a horror, the end behind which remains only nothingness, or at best a great uncertainty. Who still considers that being *permitted* to depart this earthly world may also signify the certificate for a course successfully completed, a release from the necessity of having to undergo still further earthly experiences?

If however, as this question would suggest, the interweaving threads of fate are stretched far beyond this earthlife, Justice takes on a quite different dimension, one not easily discernible to us. What has not already been perpetrated in the way of evil, outrage, and atrocity in the history of mankind?! Would it seem to us just, if a person who at one time burdened himself with such guilt were bedded on roses in a future life? Who can actually claim that within his entire earthly pilgrimage there was nothing for him to make good? Thus let us refrain from a questioning, indeed a rebellious attitude regarding events whose significance we fail to perceive, simply because we can never know the intricate paths of destiny of those concerned, including our own. Our view is mercifully veiled to enable us, unburdened by the fear of impending reactions, to change wisely and thereby to sever ourselves from old entanglements. Yet our personality, with which we entered this life, was formed by everything already experienced. That explains, by the way, the apparently so mysterious disparity of human beings even from birth.

Permit me to refrain here and now from entering more fully into the nature and origin of spirit, into its development and reincarnation. It would take all evening. [*Editor's note*. For information about other lectures by Dr. Steinpach, see addresses listed at the end of this book.] Today, above all, I wish to deal with something else, namely the question of why God appears to permit all that brings so much suffering to mankind.

One important prerequisite for dealing with this question has already been clarified. We have had to recognize that our range of vision is far too restricted and that the standards we apply are wrong because they are human-earthly. *God's* Love and *God's* Justice, however, relate to entirely different values and dimensions. The connections between events therefore may also lie beyond that which we can fathom at present. And from this arises an extremely important, fundamental realization: that where, in any particular instance, we are unable to perceive the correlation between cause and effect, which we deem necessary for the concept of Justice, it merely proves the inadequacy of our ability to judge, but by no means the absence of Justice!

Now it may seem to many an easy way out to assign the cause of any inexplicable event to some indeterminate domain. Much could be said for this proposition if we did not know about the existence of a higher, irrevocable Justice. In fact it is the awareness of this Justice in cases where it is not obvious to us that causes us to feel its absence and to ask the question: "Why?"

This knowledge has long since even become proverbial. Do we not say, "Do as you would be done by" and "As you sow, so shall you reap"? German proverbs say, "He who sets a trap for others falls into it himself" and "The echo from the woods gives back your call."

All these sayings represent experiences, which regardless of the pictures in which they are clothed, mean always the same thing: whatever has emanated from us returns to us. This recognition could only be reflected in these common sayings because it has been confirmed again and again. And this is precisely what we expect of scientific research whose results are to be considered reliable: verification through repetition! Thus on the strength of recurring experiences we can, as it were, regard it as scientifically reliable *that there is Justice.*

Of course the fact that this Justice can be established in some but not in other cases leads many people to assume that *God* acts arbitrarily. Even our manner of praying is often based on this conception. We beg Him to let or not to let this or that come to pass because for Him absolutely everything is possible (so we think). But how humanly small do we thus conceive of *God*!

Surely we are all familiar with the concept of perfection. To Whom is that word more likely to apply than to *God,* the Creator, always given that He does exist? Thus *The Grail Message* brings to our awareness only that which is actually self-evident: out of Perfection *can* proceed only what is perfect, of which absolutely nothing, simply on account of this Perfection, is subject to change. Perfection neither needs nor tolerates completion since it contains everything. This means, however, that from its very inception Creation is based upon an unchangeable order. From

10

this arises an inference that can alter radically our view of life. *The Grail Message* enlightens us about it as follows:

"*But God does not at all directly intervene in all these small and great cares of men, such as wars, misery and other earthly matters! From the very beginning He has woven into Creation His perfect Laws, which automatically carry out their incorruptible work so that all is accurately fulfilled, forever taking effect uniformly, thus preventing any preference as well as any prejudice, an injustice being impossible.*

"*Hence God has no need to trouble Himself especially about this, His Work is without flaws.*"

And now ask yourself, examine, and weigh: is this portrayal of *God* not far more exalted than the one of a God who obligingly interferes here and there and must *subsequently* set matters to rights? What miserable patchwork, ever in need of improvement, would He thus have created! The assumption that *God* could at any time proceed at will, could let one thing or another run a different course, is truly not religious greatness. Rather, this assumption of arbitrary intervention belittles and humanizes the *Godhead*, Whose Perfection is thereby denied.

That *God* does *not* "act" arbitrarily, that He is not active in every happening, demands a total rethinking for many. Yet is this really so difficult for us? In the above quote the

11

author says that *God* has woven into Creation His perfect Laws. Is that not so? Would we perhaps refute this? Does not the mechanism of Creation, does not Nature, give us the constant example of this independent working that requires no further regulating intervention by the Creator? For a long time we have had to acknowledge the existence of such Laws that cannot be influenced by men. They are the foundation of all the natural sciences. Only on the basis of these immovable Laws can we build and can science and technology develop. Like nerve fibers these Laws permeate the whole of Creation, registering everything that happens therein, good and bad, right and wrong, operating automatically. Our autonomic nervous system offers us a reduced likeness of this: independent of our will and each time in the best possible way, it controls our vital functions, such as heartbeat, respiration, digestion, adjustment by the pupil of the eye to the amount of light, or by the skin to temperature. But in spite of these automatic mechanisms, our body, due to the inscrutable movement of the heart through which the blood pulsates, is connected with the mystery of life. Creation too is no mechanically unwinding clockwork left to itself, as deism conceives of it. It is a living organism filled with the highest wisdom and constantly sustained by the Creator, from Whom alone comes movement and thereby life.

Thus the last possibility of doubt disappears. If *God* simply *cannot* act arbitrarily because of His unchangeable Laws, Whose perfection neither requires nor allows arbitrary action, there must be underlying Justice even where we are unable to recognize it.

This Justice is based on one of the three great fundamental Laws that support Creation: the *Law of Reciprocal*

*Action.* It stipulates that everything must return to its starting point. In the closing of the cycle every effect must connect by reacting upon its cause. We encounter this lawfulness in the most varied ways: in the blood-circulation, the electric circuit, the water-cycle, the rotation of atoms as well as planets, to mention only a few. We are familiar with the effects of this Law as feedback; we make use of it in computer technology and allow for it in "recycling." The above-cited proverbs, expressing wisdom gained by experience, such as "Do as you would be done by," testify that this same lawfulness also includes connections whose cause is within the human *will,* that is, in the *spiritual.*

Why then do we shrink from acknowledging this simple fact of which we have so long been aware? Let us admit that our arrogance, our conceit, stands in the way of this realization, for we would then have to admit that it is from ourselves at some time, in this life or another, that something once emanated that now falls back upon us. But of course it is much easier and more pleasant to blame another, especially the Creator, for one's own mistakes and then to ask how He could permit them.

In truth, however, *we* are unjust towards Him when posing questions like these or asking: "What of Justice?" Exactly as the corresponding symbol appears at the touch of a typewriter key, so in the immutable lawfulness of Creation we ourselves release the very effects that we then complain about. Today computer technology allows us an even better understanding of this. Like commands in a computer program, these lawful principles are stored in Creation. There are countless possibilities offered to the user of the program. But the answer that results will always be based on the Programmer.

Thus we see that the tables are turned. It is not *God* who decides what may be in store for us; it is *we* ourselves who are responsible for what will and must strike us sooner or later in this or in a future life as a result of the *Creation Law of Reciprocal Action.*

*Must* strike us! Is it then a cruel, vengeful God, who, instead of leniently and lovingly forgiving us our failings, also permits suffering to come upon us through the Law He has placed in Creation?

We are back with the question to which we originally turned our thoughts: "Why the suffering?" "What is its meaning?" Perhaps we should also ask: "Why do we cling to the unpleasant?" "Why is it that only the dark sides of life induce us to ask such questions?" After all, it is the same *Law of Reciprocal Action* that also bestows well-being, joy, and prosperity. These pleasant experiences, however, we take for granted without asking why they come to us and what meaning lies within them.

With this simple thought we have taken another great step towards clarification. Neither a vengeful *God* nor His merciless Law have intended suffering for us. Through the Law of God we could and should actually receive only what is joyful. Hence what constitutes the difference?

At this decisive point we can only proceed slowly, in small steps; we do not want to lose our footing. Therefore let me go back to the simple illustration of touching the key of a typewriter. Let us assume you struck the wrong key. It means that you made a mistake. You have produced something other than what is right. The self-evident consequence will be that you have to correct that mistake. Just let us learn from the small things, from the everyday occurrences of life! For they bear within them the same

14

lawful principles, though modified, that apply also to the great events.

Now let us take a further step into an even larger sphere of activity. The laws we enact within a political system indeed express the will of the lawmaker, we all realize that. On the basis of this analogy, we may draw the corresponding conclusion that the immovable Laws of Creation proceeding from the Creator reveal His unchanging Will.

This Will, contained within the Laws, therefore regulates what is right, what is to be, what may be. That can always be only what corresponds to this Will, never what opposes it. We now also have the reply to the unanswered question: "What is good?" Alas, good is mostly not what we, subjectively, regard as such; good can always be only that which objectively complies with the Laws of Creation! That means, whenever we do something that runs counter to these Laws, to *God's* Will, we have made a mistake, as in the above illustration, and must consequently remedy it.

Now to avoid stumbling over the laws of the land in earthly life, we must be informed about them. But what do we do regarding the Laws of Creation? In the "*Lord's Prayer*" we say: "Lord, *Thy* Will be done on earth as it is in Heaven." Surely, rightly understood, that is not a petition: it is meant to be a solemn promise! For what obstacle stands in the way? His Will surrounds us in the Laws of Creation. It is *we* who through our contrary volition wreak havoc in this earthly world! Yet if I were to ask you how we can know *God's* Will, Whose unobstructed continuity *we* should ensure, who among you would be able to give an answer?

Hence we must also seek to know the Laws of the great system, "Creation," in which we live. But how are we to go about it? We cannot read them in some book of statutes. They are inherent, however, in the whole of Creation, where their effects are made evident. That is the language in which the Creator speaks to us, and which, as is apparent in regard to our sins against the environment, we begin but belatedly and gradually to understand.

How do we teach a creature who does not, or does not yet, understand our language how he is to conduct himself, what he is or is not to do? The undisputed means of even the most loving education is to help him realize what is right or wrong through experiencing the pleasant or the unpleasant. Joy and suffering are but the instruments of such an education meant to develop the understanding of right behavior. Suffering is nothing other than the consequence of individual or collective wrong conduct, that is, non-observance of the Laws of Creation. The hardships under which people now suffer as a result of poisoned air, water, and food demonstrate this quite plainly. These certainly did not arise at the Creator's behest through a maliciousness of Nature; we human beings have brought about this state of affairs!

When our public system of justice passes sentence upon a person who breaks the law, the purpose is twofold. On the one hand, in keeping with our conception of justice, we see in it an atonement, a restitution; on the other, the punishment seeks to reform. Experience of the unpleasant should lead the perpetrator to an understanding of the wrong committed so that in the future he will refrain from it. In the final analysis love is the mainspring, intended to spare the individual concerned further injury, although

16

this is something we seldom understand. Thereby our judicial system again simply reflects what also exists in the order of Creation.

Indeed, it is made so easy for us to understand this. Let us call to mind again the automatic vital functions in our bodies, such as respiration, heartbeat, digestion, and adaptation to light and temperature. Man can disrupt this best possible order. Through overexertion you can develop heart trouble; if you have overeaten, you may become sick; if you look into glaring light, you are blinded; if you lie in the sun too long, you are sunburned. Every time you suffer some degree of discomfort. How does this come about? The self-acting lawful principles have responded to your wrong conduct; they have reacted. At the same time, this pattern contains a loving reminder: you must not do that! From these experiences in the small intelligible world of your physical body, you can perceive the same interplay that takes place everywhere throughout Creation. Therefore, you can understand how these lawful principles give rise to every type of suffering, whose ultimate purpose is always and only a loving one. To contemplate this process in its all-embracing magnitude, we must first deal more fully with how man's influence affects Creation. We must recognize Creation as ultimately a continuous alternation of vibrations brought about by the sustaining Radiation of God, which for its part is nothing other than vibration. "The whole universe," writes Fritjof Capra, a nuclear physicist and one of many who could be quoted, "manifests in a multiplicity of vibrations of varying frequencies." (*The Turning Point*, Bantam, 1987). Even decades ago science established that material substance does not actually exist at all. What we regard as such, what appears

17

to us as solid form, is essentially only condensed energy, in brief, a parcel of vibrations. Man constantly influences these fields of vibration. Not only his actions, but even his thoughts and volitions, produce vibrations that take on forms corresponding exactly with their nature. Here the second of the great basic Laws of Creation, the *Law of Attraction of Homogeneous Species*, becomes manifest. We know it in the physical world as resonance: the tendency of everything tuned to the same pitch to vibrate sympathetically. It is the basis of homeopathy, based on the principle of like affecting like. We see this great Law in the spiritual realm when people of similar interests find each other. Here the vibrations emanating from one individual connect with homogeneous vibrations, strengthening these vibrations, and, in turn, are strengthened by them. This explains the Biblical words: "They have sown the wind, and they shall reap the whirlwind."

According to the *Law of Reciprocal Action*, at the closing of the cycle the vibrations that emanated from a human being return to him, strengthened by the homogeneous species. Just as in the examples in the physical world, these returning vibrations correspond exactly to the nature or character of what has been "put into the world" by him. Thus he now experiences in concentrated form how he gladdened others or what he did to hurt them. It becomes apparent that incorruptible Justice lies in these Laws!

If life brings us joy and happiness, we may accept these experiences gratefully, since they too by no means fall to our lot undeserved. How meaningful is the following: in our joy we would like to "embrace the whole world"; we would like to do good to everyone; or in our bliss over some unexpected help, we would like to help others in turn. The inspiration, the power, bestowed upon us through some genuine experience of happiness is unmistakable and in it lies *spiritual* advancement, which we experience through the Law of Creation.

Now, I hope, you will also understand the meaning that lies in suffering, the result of this principle of action and reaction. The wrong once perpetrated against the Law of Creation, the Will of God, must be redressed. Having taken on form, it has been stored in the Program of Creation; its presence there disrupts the harmonious running. Now, let us say, if you wish to erase a recording from a tape, simply a vibration given form and preserved, or replace it with another, you must let the tape run again past the "sound-head," thus bringing about the closing of a cycle. A volition emanating from the spirit also requires a spiritual closing of the cycle. Only by returning to its starting point can it be effaced as a vibration.

On account of previous individual life paths, each human spirit is unique, different from any other. This uniqueness is expressed down to the very finger tips— think of the fingerprint. The vibration emanating from a spirit, from his personality, cannot therefore be erased by another, as with a sound-head, but solely by *himself.* Only the spirit in its uniqueness possesses the requisite "code." Thereby the originator alone can bring about release from this entanglement, from the "karma" burdening him. Of course, this requires the acceptance of suffering, which would otherwise strike him anew on some other occasion. But the question: "Why should I suffer such a blow of fate?" is a protest. It demonstrates a lack of understanding, a failure to acknowledge *oneself* as the originator of what has now condensed into a redeeming event.

To understand, one must not necessarily apprehend the starting point and the connection. They may indeed lie in an earlier life, still wisely veiled from us. What is decisive in any case is solely the recognition of *personal* causality, based on Divine Justice. It is a kind of spiritual final examination, demanding of us the only thing we need: *the understanding of the Creation Laws and their ever solely helpful significance.* As soon as you begin to think in terms of this other dimension, the pressure of suffering subsides and you see that you yourself caused it, by your rebellion or your opposition. The cycle can now close, and you can experience a liberation. Have human beings not experienced countless times that just through suffering they have grown spiritually in an unforeseen manner, gaining a new attitude to life and casting off much wrong? Thus suffering is no longer sorrowful to the afflicted but a source of inner strength. You now see that even in suffering one realizes the truth, expressed in *The Grail Message* and quoted earlier, that "Divine Love weaves only what *benefits* the human *spirit.*" In other words, Divine Love helps him achieve the purpose of his existence, which lies in making fully conscious use of his spiritual potential for the benefit of Creation.

Since this possibility is inherent in any kind of suffering, there is no "useless" life, one which could be obliterated or cast away. Nor are there any "mentally handicapped" persons. Only the instrument, the physical body, is impaired so that the indwelling spirit cannot be fully effective on earth. It suffers under this incapacity, under this disabled instrument of communication, but it experiences as does any other spirit. With the proper insight it can release itself from what, in any case, is heavy guilt.

Now many a person may well fear the effect of such reciprocal action. But how lovingly indeed are we cared for! In wonderfully consoling words *The Grail Message* tells us:

"*You need not be sad and depressed! At any moment you can set out on your way to the Height and make good the past, whatever it may be.*"

After all, we need not wait until the reciprocal action strikes us with full force. There is nothing to prevent our changing for the good even before it comes to that. What takes place in this case will seem to you absolutely self-evident, if you recollect what I told you earlier about the vibrations. As the author of *The Grail Message* describes the process:

"*Now if a person has cultivated within himself an honest good volition, it follows that also the layer surrounding him will be of a like nature. Returning reciprocal actions of an evil nature, dating from former times, are now held up by this layer opposing them, and diverted or absorbed and disintegrated before they are able to strike the person himself; they are thus either completely eliminated or at least considerably weakened, so that through his earnest good volition he has thereby received forgiveness for the former evil.*"

21

In physics this effect is known as "interference." If two different vibrations meet, they cancel each other out in the same way as wave crests and troughs in opposition are mutually weakened or even obliterated. In this connection *The Grail Message* speaks of "symbolic redemption." The closing of the cycle takes place in any case, but through an event, which because of a change of heart already undergone, will no longer appear arduous to the one concerned. Thus it is again *we* who are in control. The effect of Justice always adapts to our spiritual condition; it takes into account the insight we have already gained.

Now I can well imagine that one or another among you would have liked a long while ago to remonstrate, "You claim that we ourselves are responsible for everything. That surely presupposes the ability to make decisions, hence that we possess free will. But just that is controversial." Well, there can scarcely be a more fitting example of the human tendency to complicate the most simple thing. To him who knows *The Grail Message* it is incomprehensible that people still engage in philosophical speculation about the freedom of will. It is quite simple: we are free to decide but are bound to the consequences of this decision. Indeed, we experience them day in and day out in everything we do. Let us imagine the following: you come out of your house and go to the left. You have thereby availed yourself of the possibility to determine which way to go. If it then occurs to you that you should rather have turned right, there is nothing to prevent you from doing so. But the new decision does not relieve you of the necessity of walking back over the distance already covered. As you can therefore see, free will and constraint exist side by side.

I also do not wish to evade a further question that will certainly come to you, should you reflect on what you have heard: "Can a person not be the victim of a misdeed without reciprocal activity being involved?" Surely everything must have had a beginning at some time!

Well, just as lightning always takes the path of least resistance, an evil will first and foremost strike him, who often unconsciously, through his thoughts, his fears, or the absence of trust in *God,* has weakened his resistance, has pierced, as it were, his spiritual armor. His attitude is already one of anticipation and, as in the case of resonance and according to the *Primordial Creation-Law of the Attraction of Homogeneous Species,* he thereby draws to himself the dreaded evil.

One must also bear in mind that here good and evil in various gradations coexist, which is a characteristic of this earthly world. This diversity serves to further spiritual development, but it calls for spiritual alertness and, as with every animal, earthly vigilance as well. Behind these needs is the *Primordial Creation-Law of Movement.* It is a compelling challenge to everything that does not wish to fall behind in its development. He who relaxes in this regard becomes vulnerable, just as the weakest animal in a herd, unable to keep pace with the rest, is snatched by a prowling beast of prey. It is no different in the spiritual either. In neither case is it a question of guilt by the one concerned, for through his weakness he only harms himself. Nevertheless, he thereby becomes the victim of a happening that he should have understood as a summons to awaken.

We should always realize that there is a *fundamental* significance, an *ever-present* meaning, in suffering, whatever its nature and origin. Ignorant of the connections, which even in the world of thoughts, may extend right into the spiritual, we are never able to distinguish between the beginning and the closing of a cycle. For who indeed knows the thoughts of another person? The long duration of human history and the repeated earth-lives already completed by everyone make it likely that reciprocal action must be considered as a primary factor. You see, there is no arbitrariness anywhere; all things are lawfully connected.

With respect to justice, then, we must proceed not from the individual event but from the lawfulness manifested therein. This demand is by no means so unusual as it may seem at first. After all, the concept is familiar to us in various fields of knowledge. In physics we speak of "half-life." We know when half the atoms of a substance will have disintegrated, but we do not know when each individual atom will disintegrate. We have statistics on mortality, indicating that a given percentage of a certain age group will pass away, but not which of them it will be. With the individual atom or human being, we are again faced with the question: "Why?" Despite common assumptions, the inscrutable individual case is unmistakably embedded in a lawfulness that becomes apparent through its effects and is only recognizable itself as supreme order.

A recent branch of physics, chaos research, has already identified this as something fundamental: there is a "sensitive order," which owing to its sensitivity to a multitude of differing influences, leads to an inordinate profusion of unpredictable results. This "sensitive order," however, is nothing other than a manifestation of the all-perceiving, self-acting Laws of Creation.

Let us then extend our view to incorporate this comprehensive understanding: the automatically-working Laws of Creation bring to us, whether joy or suffering, always only what at some time in this or in a former life corresponded to our will or to our nature deriving from this will.

That certainly changes all previous conceptions. It dispels the concept of punishment. *God* does not punish. Rather, through His Laws He simply grants the fulfillment of our wishes, even if they are intended for others! That this fulfillment frequently is disagreeable to us is due solely to the nature of these wishes; we are thus meant to realize the error of our ways. Rightly considered, then, there is only one thing that we must fear: ourselves!

Thus the author of *The Grail Message* shows us a new, gladdening picture of the world. He says:

"*Do you now understand the great simplicity that lies in the whole of the world happening? Whatever happens therein, it can always only be love!*"

I am well aware that with so many terrible things in this world it is not easy to recognize love as the only true primal cause. But from whence originates this wonderful intuitive perception called love, which every one of us is able to experience, if not from the Creator, the Origin of all that exists? *God is Love*, and therefore only Love can emanate from Him! That this is not an ecstatic conception, but the reality of Creation, has quite recently been confirmed by death research. People who had already been considered clinically dead but came back to life have almost all reported that the first and strongest impression in the disembodied state had been one of overwhelming, unutterable love!

From this understanding arises our own task: we must transform and pass on this love. The suffering of others offers us an opportunity to do so. It would be wrong to leave the sufferer helpless on the assumption that his fate is self-inflicted. True help, however, must include the spiritual; it must elucidate the full context of what has happened for the sufferer. In this way suffering gains in importance: it can become a challenge for the afflicted to improve themselves, enabling them in their turn to make good many things. Consider that this earth, to whose creation we have contributed absolutely nothing, gives us all that we need for our existence. The great *Primordial Creation-Law of Reciprocal Action*, which is at the same time the *Law of Equilibrium*, does not, however, tolerate one-sided taking. But what do we have to offer in return? With the right help extended to our fellow creature, we give love to him and ourselves at the same time; we become useful, promoting the spiritual purpose of our existence. Here is the counter-value that *we* are able to give—*effective gratitude* for the omnipresent Love of the Creator!

This Love, which is simultaneously helpful Justice, surrounds us even before birth. It is neither a matter of chance nor arbitrariness that determines into which environment and to which parents we are born. Again the two previously-mentioned great Primordial Laws of Creation are decisive for this. If there still exist fateful entanglements from former lives, which must be severed in the

26

closing of the cycle, the *Law of Reciprocal Action* will lead those involved together. Otherwise, the *Law of Attraction of Homogeneous Species* arranges for the incorporation of the human spirit where—remember the concept of resonance—it finds a similar *spiritual* condition. The concept of "relationship" indeed refers to this similarity. This law enables the spirit to continue developing in its own way. This is particularly evident in generations of artists, where the artistic abilities are often incorrectly viewed as resulting from heredity. By including the concepts of spirit and reincarnation, one can see clearly that spiritual qualities can neither be handed down nor inherited. They are the result of totally differing experiences and empirical knowledge gained by a human spirit on the paths of its past existence. They constitute its personality, with which it is born anew. Heredity therefore is restricted to physical features. Similar tendencies and abilities between parents and children are due to the attraction of homogeneous species. Now you can see that through the working of the Laws of Creation, even at birth, the spirit is offered what corresponds to it and what it needs for its further development.

This loving solicitude extends also beyond death. The finer covering worn by the spirit after laying aside its physical body is lighter or heavier depending on the degree to which a human being has bound himself to coarser earthly matter (see *Why We Live After Death?* by Richard Steinpach, available from the addresses listed at the end of this book). Now an additional Primordial Law of Creation, the *Law of Gravity*, takes effect. We know that what is light rises and what is heavy sinks. In centrifuging, this separating effect can be quite clearly recognized. Just as it can be observed on earth, in water, and in the air, so also in the beyond this Law operates to sort and distribute what is of similar weight. It compels those of a like nature to be together. These human spirits create for each other worlds of joyful or sorrowful experiences. A light spirit, who has become luminous, is furthered by his homogeneous surroundings; a heavier one, still bound to the Darkness, will be induced to achieve understanding and change by personally experiencing in others his own ill-nature directed against himself, filling him with loathing.

Thus we are always led by Justice and Love. The Laws of *God* instructively ensure that some fleeting deceptive advantage does not cause us to lose the way to our true happiness. Again it is we ourselves who have wrongly pictured the Love of *God*. It is not indulgent, weakly complying with everything, as we would have it in support of our wrong conduct; it is demanding, thereby furthering and purposeful! His magnanimity, His mercy, and His forgiveness lie in the opportunities offered in the Laws of Creation that enable us to free ourselves from all entanglements. But as stated before, nobody else could and can do this for us: not even the *Son of God.* He could only show us the paths that the Laws provide for us and to which we must then, of course, adhere.

Perhaps you have already noticed how naturally I have spoken of *God* throughout, although at the beginning of the lecture I raised the question as to His very existence. The answer to this question, which we find in *The Grail Message*, is actually of a compelling simplicity:

*"*W*hether you say: I voluntarily submit to the existing Laws of Nature because it is for my own good, or: I submit to God's Will, Which manifests in the Laws of Nature, or to the unfathomable Power which activates the Laws of Nature... would the effect be any different? The Power is there and you acknowledge it, you simply must acknowledge it, because as soon as you reflect a little there is nothing else you can do... and thereby you acknowledge your God, the Creator!"*

All our doubts, then, actually concern the intelligibility of a concept whose active reality we *must* acknowledge, whether we like it or not. Our doubts are justified, for He will always be inconceivable to us. After all, we are but one of the countless creatures permitted to awaken to consciousness out of His Radiation. A part can never grasp the complete whole! In the course of our spiritual development we can only gain a growing understanding of His Will, which lies in the Laws of Creation, and thus draw nearer to Him, *experiencing* Him ever more clearly through this knowledge. How beautifully Goethe has "condensed" this in verse:

*As you rise aloft to higher spheres,*
*Growing always and behold:*
*How pure, eternal, God appears*
*Ever stronger to unfold.*
*For the spirits' sustentation in the freest*
*    firmament this:*

*Love Eternal's revelation*
*That becomes eternal bliss."*

This is no poetic exaltation. It gives expression to the intuitive longing, rooted in the spirit, to achieve the goal of its existence! Then let us open the way for the spirit to attain it!

If we now would reflect upon what we can do for the liberation of the spirit, let us again start with what is simple. Briefly, I have contended that we ourselves are invariably the cause of everything that strikes us. After a little reflection you will observe that this is actually nothing new. "All are architects of Fate," says the poet; and proverb says that "Heaven and hell lie within one's own breast." That is surely founded on the same recognition. But what does it mean? It simply proves that the foregoing explanations are correct! We have found and still find this understanding confirmed by the experience that has become proverbial. Although we should long ago have accepted this truth, it has obviously made no impression upon us, for otherwise we simply could not ask questions such as how *God* can permit all the adversity. Indeed we should long since have known the answer. Let us be honest: we would not accept the knowledge; we have suppressed it. And we believed that we were justified in doing so because we lacked the knowledge that conveys absolute certainty. That is how it is, not otherwise!

In any case, since the time of Copernicus and Galileo we have lived in a state of confusion, which is called somewhat ironically the "Two-World Theory." On the one hand, there is the world of faith, full of human interpretations, which holds that even what is contrary to Natural Law is possible. It must be accepted "blindly," that is, without being understood and with the comforting assurance of the belief that nothing is impossible because of *God's* Omnipotence. Man does not, indeed will not, see the imperfection thereby imputed to His Work.

On the other hand, there is the world of natural science in which the immovable validity of lawful principles has become so obvious that the deeply religious physicist, Pascal Jordan, felt obliged to state that "Even for any religious person the truth is irrefutable that *God* in no way reveals His Omnipotence by continually infringing against the Laws of Nature" (*Der Naturwissenschaftler vor der religiosen Frage*, Stalling-Verlag). And the biologist Rupert Riedl underscored this constraint with the words: "*God* also observes the Laws made by Him, and these Laws are inviolable. They must be observed" (*Der Gottheit lebendiges Kleid*, Verlag Franz Deuticke). These two conflicting worldviews have not hitherto been bridged, nor can they be. Now people do not know which is valid. The support that provides certainty is lacking.

But the man of today wants to be able to *understand*! Nothing else is of any help or use either! And in this lies the distinguishing feature of the profoundly significant work I have quoted: Belief can now become *knowledge*!

I gave you an example of this before. Long-familiar observations, which we could previously only acknowledge as facts, we can now discern as the fundamentally intelligible effects of Law. With a little reflection, you realize that you can trace back and explain all processes, both of material and spiritual natures, by the Primordial Laws of Creation discussed above. In view of their significance I will mention them again and give you something by which to remember them. The *Law of Gravity* works from

31

above downwards, as it were: picture it simply as a vertical line. The *Law of Attraction of Homogeneous Species* unites on the same plane those things that correspond to each other: hence, picture it as a horizontal line. Finally, the *Law of Reciprocal Action* links beginning and end in the closing of a cycle: this would be consistent with a circle. Picture as a symbol an equal-armed cross in a ring, and you can see the three incontestable Primordial Laws of Creation, the all-creating Living Truth in the ancient symbol of faith.

These three basic Laws are nothing but forms of activity of a single instigating factor: *movement*. Movement brought about by the sustaining Radiation Pressure of *God*. Indeed, everything in Creation is movement, from the orbit of the planets to the atoms; there is no standstill anywhere. This movement demands that we go with it, for only in movement is there life: just think of the heartbeat. The proverb "He who rests, rusts" refers in its all-embracing validity not only to the necessity for physical activity but even more so to spiritual development. In this, our life's task, we must progress in order to avoid remaining behind in the insistent movement of Creation and losing all meaning in our earthly labors.

To develop the spirit! The linguistic origins of the word indicate what is required. It involves detaching the spirit from all entanglements, laying bare and freeing what is innermost, the essence. We can do this only with the help of the Truth. It is Truth that we must learn how to perceive. Only then will we begin to comprehend how we must conduct ourselves.

Every thinking man perceives intuitively that there can be only one single Truth. "What is Truth?" was, however, the question derisively and doubtingly asked, even by Pilate, when Jesus spoke of It. And until now this uncertainty makes the quest for Truth seem futile to many people. I too, I openly admit it, was very skeptical when for the first time I read the exacting title of this book *In the Light of Truth*. But the misgivings disappeared quite soon, for through this book we learn to understand that Truth *is!* Alive and active in and about us, It surrounds us and must be evident in everything. Thus It is always visible to us. Why then do we not see It? The path to It is opened not by philosophical speculation but solely through understanding the lawful principles underlying all happenings!

And how easy it is to understand these lawful principles in their matchless simplicity! The author of *The Grail Message* says:

"*It all lies so simply before man that owing to the very simplicity they often do not come to recognition, because from the outset they assume that the great work of Creation must be much more difficult and intricate.*"

In nature we see that this is actually so. Is not everything there always so adjusted as to achieve the best possible result in the quickest, simplest, and most economical way? In such a way as to have prompted one of the most distinguished physicists of our time to ask, "How did we actually discover simple Laws, when Nature is so complex?" [*Bild der Wissenschaft*, Nr. 2/86, S. 66 (DVA)]. And these Laws, as scientists have established everywhere, exist not

33

only in Nature but in *all* outward manifestations of life, thus also of spiritual life. Please realize what this means!

How simple this recognition makes the way to a true understanding of how Creation works. From this understanding, however, it follows, again expressed quite simply, that we must conform to these Laws! If we do not observe them *we* pronounce *our own* judgment!

For this reason the author of *The Grail Message* has no need to prove anything to us in the usual way. With sovereign clarity he says: that is how it is! And he calls upon us to look about ourselves in order to become convinced of the rightness of his words. We must, so he says, "find the Message again in life, for it speaks to us out of life." And indeed, we find it there, and one new insight, one "aha-experience," will follow another; and thereby what you have heard or read can, indeed *must*, become a certainty.

To illustrate this, I would like to give an example. If a firm pollutes the environment through its emissions, we consider it quite proper that it be held responsible for rectifying the wrong it has brought about. The labor and cost involved present an inconvenience and a burden for the owner that will at the same time induce him to avoid emitting harmful substances in the future. Here we have observed an occurrence in life—and have you noticed something? All at once the Law of Reciprocal Action and the meaning of suffering in all their logical simplicity become clear to us. On the higher plane we can see rectification according to the principle of causality: elimination of the harmful spiritual emissions that a man has created through wrong thinking and volition and that have polluted Creation. And as in the earthly example, the reciprocal effect fulfills the same dual purpose!

My statement early in the lecture that "whatever happens, it can only be love" may now hopefully be more understandable to you. Whoever lives according to the Laws of Creation, or *God's* Will, experiences directly the support inherent in these Laws. Whoever violates the Laws because of a false volition, weakness, or indolence receives through these same Laws the opportunity to be released from his guilt and also to be roused to wakefulness. Always the Laws direct him back onto the right path. To further the development of the human spirit so that we constantly gain a better understanding of *God's* Will is fundamental to everything. True Love, the *Love of God*, is directed only to this end!

This simplicity, which knowledge of the Laws of Creation reveals everywhere in life, enables us to follow the explanations of the author of *The Grail Message* even into realms and heights presently inaccessible to us. There too we encounter the same universally-valid Laws, whose effects we perceive here on earth in the most commonplace happenings and in the most amazing discoveries.

Let me offer this out of my personal experience. As a lawyer previously little concerned with natural science, I became fascinated by how scientific discoveries, which today are accessible even to the layman, suddenly became highly interesting and intelligible when I was able to view them as confirming *The Grail Message*. Indeed, even where science simply establishes facts without being able to interpret them, *The Grail Message* provides the explanation. This extends to the most spectacular discoveries of recent times. Thus research on dying, on the brain, the laser beam and holography that is based upon it, even the discovery by astrophysics of "black holes" caused by the dissolution of stars through extreme densification, all these have always only proved fundamentally correct what is stated in *The Grail Message* regarding these various phenomena. Yet until the time some sixty years ago when this work was written all this was not only totally unknown, but in part even inconceivable.

With full justification *The Grail Message* can therefore demand:

"*The philosophy of religion and the philosophy of natural science must in every respect coincide in perfect clarity and consistency if they are to represent the Truth!*"

Here in this work this unity is established!

Therefore I am pained when I see the confused manner in which questions about human existence are speculated upon or guessed at in lectures or in radio and television discussions. I would then like to call to the participants, "Read this book *In the Light of Truth*!" You would find in it all the answers! But to be able to read it, man must first know of its existence. And that is the sole reason for my presentation. After all, I am neither a preacher nor a missionary. I act on behalf of no one. I am simply a human being, who now advanced in years, wishes to convey the happy experiences of decades to those, who like myself at one time, are searching for Truth, those who nowadays are becoming ever more numerous.

Basically, I would like to say to you only this: there is this book that is so helpful, which removes our doubts and enables our spirit to have freedom of vision. What you do with this suggestion is entirely your concern. It is of no profit to me. Even the author of *The Grail Message* wrote:

"*I* *offer to the seekers, but I do not solicit ... I do not seek to 'persuade' a single person ... Whoever does not want my Word has only to leave it alone. After all, I do not force it on anyone.*"

But meanwhile, there is the force of circumstances that compels us to occupy ourselves with it. The very concept "force of circumstances" is an alarming revelation of how far we have carried things: we have become slaves of our self-created institutions, which instead of serving us, now rule us. Here we experience the *Law of Reciprocal Action.* How could it come to this?

When on the highway a driver comes toward us against the flow of traffic, we cry out, "Is he mad? He is endangering himself and others!" But like such drivers, we have persistently driven in the wrong direction, against the living current of the Laws of Creation. Now we complain about the things that befall us or, better said, that go against us: the suffering of the individual, of peoples, indeed of all mankind, who destroy their own living foundations by disregarding the greatest of all "traffic regulations," those of Creation.

Yet what a magnificent, stupendous, meaningful time we live in! We sense something approaching us irresistibly, capable of bringing about a radical change in our prevailing mode of living. Indeed, we know that things cannot continue as they are. Otherwise we are rushing open-eyed towards destruction. We stand at a Cosmic Turning-Point, more significant than that which once divested man of his delusion of grandeur, his regarding himself as the center of Creation. This Cosmic Turning-Point *enforces* a new *spiritual* beginning. This explains the spread of confusion, menace, and horror in our world of today. So much that is still wrong must experience the closing of its cycle, must be lived to completion to be "effaced," in order to prepare the soil for a new and wiser way of living. Already the dawn of this new time is gradually becoming discernible. But what is germinating as we begin this contemplation? Our becoming conscious of the *responsibility we bear towards Creation,* and thus for ourselves! By our wrong, selfish desires we have wrought havoc, disruption, and destruction wherever we turn. Now we must learn to adapt ourselves. This, you see, is precisely the point that I have spoken about all evening and, which at the same time, contains the answer to the question posed in the title of this lecture!

What does it avail us to know that so much, in fact everything prevailing until now, has been wrong if we cannot find a solution and do not yet know what is better? It is as if the author of *The Grail Message* takes us lovingly by the hand when he says,

"*I* bring a Message to which men can cling in order to extricate themselves from their errors."

Precisely within this Message lies the help that we need today!

Yet even now I hear the objection of those who would say, "That is fine and not wrong either. But why do we need this book? After all, we have the Bible, we have Jesus. He has already brought us the Message telling us how to live an upright life!"

In principle they are right, of course. But then we read in John 16:12 the words of Jesus, heavy with deep pain, at the Last Supper: "I have yet many things to say unto you, but ye cannot bear them now." In other words, "ye cannot" absorb or understand them. Why do people not think more deeply about these words? Is it not shocking that He, the *Son of God*, Who had come to show us the right way, was dependent upon the ability of a few human spirits to comprehend, and that consequently we could receive of His Message only what passed through the filter of their comprehension? He could not have lamented more clearly that His Mission had remained piecework, that through His early, violent death—remember His cry: "Father, forgive them, for they know not what they do!" (Luke 23:24)—it remained incomplete. He therefore announced that He would send *another* Comforter, the Spirit of Truth, Who would guide us into *all* Truth. That promise would not have been necessary had it been possible for Jesus to bring us the whole Truth. This *other one*, so He said, "shall take of mine." Hence He would link up with Jesus' Word, "speak," "bring to your remembrance," "teach," and "testify," and "the Judgment would be with Him." (John 14:16-17, 26; 15:26; 16:7-8, 13-15). That certainly cannot be connected with the Pentecostal experience of the disciples, as it has been interpreted. (This is something quite different, which *The Grail Message* also explains.)

Nor do the words of Jesus refer to an impersonal Power bestowed upon the disciples that brought no supplementary Truth and certainly not the Judgment. Instead these words describe clearly the activity of a *Person*. The disciples themselves did not take it to be otherwise, for some time afterwards Paul wrote in his first Epistle to the Corinthians (13:9-10), "For we know in part.... But when that which is perfect is come, then that which is in part shall be done away." Thus the fulfillment of the promise still remained open.

Since then surely every generation is called upon to seek this expanded, supplementary Truth. Where can it be found? Who will bring it to us? The real question should be: "What more would and could we expect than a view of the world that explains the origin and purpose of Creation and which, by showing us its Laws, gives us the knowledge necessary for our human existence?!" What more can we ask, finally, than a view of the world, which as far as the horizon of recognition extends, is in full accord with the natural sciences and in which Jesus, free from all errors that have entwined His Person and His Teaching, will at last obtain His true Majesty as the *Son of God*?!

But understand me correctly: far be it from me to make a definite assertion. Each person must examine for himself. Nobody else can do it for you. Only the intuitive perception, the language of your spirit, can tell you whose word we are dealing with here....

If you have questions about the content of this lecture,
please contact Reader Services at:

GRAIL
FOUNDATION PRESS
14318 Shirley Bohn Rd.
Mt. Airy, MD 21771
1-800-427-9217

Abd-ru-shin. 1990. *In the Light of Truth: The Grail Message.* Stuttgart: Stiftung Gralsbotschaft

Abd-ru-shin. 1990. *The Ten Commandments of God and The Lord's Prayer.* Stuttgart: Stiftung Gralsbotschaft

*Bild der Wissenschaft.* Nr. 2/86, S. 66 (DVA)

Capra, Fritjof. 1987. *The Turning Point.* New York: Bantam

Jordan, Pascal. *Der Naturwissenschaftler vor der religiosen Frage.* Stalling-Verlag

Riedl, Rupert. *Der Gottheit lebendiges Kleid.* Verlag Franz Deuticke

Steinpach, Richard. 1995. *Why We Live After Death.* Gambier, Ohio: Grail Foundation Press

*r. Richard Steinpach was born in Vienna in 1917 where he was a lawyer for forty years. His professional life provided extensive opportunities to observe human nature, and to deal with many life-questions and problems. Between 1979 and 1991, he gave hundreds of lectures throughout Germany, Austria, and Switzerland. The powerful response of his audiences convinced him to publish his manuscripts in book form. Dr. Steinpach died in 1992.*

## *In The Light Of Truth: The Grail Message*
### An Introduction

*I*N THE LIGHT OF TRUTH: THE GRAIL MESSAGE
*is a classic work that offers clear and perceptive
answers to questions which challenge every human
being. Written between the years 1923-1938, it is
a collection of 168 lectures addressing all spheres of
life ranging from life after death to God and the Universe,
the Laws in Creation, free will, intuition and the intellect,
the ethereal world and the beyond, justice and love. It
answers eternal questions such as what does it mean to be
human, what is the purpose of life on earth, and what happens to "me" when I die.* In the Light of Truth: The Grail
Message *explains the causes and significance of the unprecedented crises facing humanity, and our responsibilities to the
future.*

*The author, Abd-ru-shin, was born in 1875 in Bischof-
swerda, Germany. His given name was Oskar Ernst Bernhardt. After being educated and trained in business, he
established himself in Dresden and became financially successful. In the years that followed, he made many journeys
abroad, and wrote successful travel books, stories and plays.*

*After residing for some time in New York, Mr. Bernhardt
journeyed to England, and in 1913, moved to London.*

*There, the outbreak of World War I took him unawares, and in 1914 he was interned on the Isle of Man.*

*The seclusion of internment brought with it an inner deepening. He reflected continuously over questions connected with the meaning of life, birth and death, responsibility and free will, and with God and Creation. More and more the desire awakened within him to help humanity. He was released in the Spring of 1919 and returned to Germany.*

*In the 1920s, Abd-ru-shin gave public lectures. His explanation of the Knowledge of Creation resounded among his hearers. He began to write the first lectures for* In the Light of Truth: The Grail Message *in 1923.*

*In 1928, Abd-ru-shin settled in Austria on a mountain plateau called Vomperberg, where he continued writing* The Grail Message. *The seizure of power in Austria by the Nazis in 1938 ended his work there. On March 12 of that year he was arrested, and his land and property were appropriated without compensation. In September, he was placed under house arrest, first in Schlauroth near Görlitz, and later in Kipsdorf in the Erzgebirge, where he was constantly under surveillance by the Gestapo. He was forbidden any further work for making* The Grail Message *known publicly.*

*On December 6, 1941, Abd-ru-shin died from the effects of these measures.*

*In 1991, upon the fiftieth anniversary of his death, the* Dresdner Nachrichten *newspaper published an article that included:*

*"*THE GRAIL MESSAGE, *which Oskar Ernst Bernhardt began to write in 1923 in Dresden, has now been translated*

*into almost all the civilized languages of the western hemisphere, and is available ... around the globe. It was forbidden in the 'Third Reich,' but was also on the list of banned literature in East Germany. These periods of prohibition (in East Germany more than fifty years) markedly curtailed the possibility of disseminating* The Grail Message *and making it known. One wonders why a non-political book like* The Grail Message *was still regarded by political systems as a 'source of danger.' The reason, perhaps, is that it sets up personal awareness of responsibility and individual freedom of choice against all conformity. Furthermore dogmatic limitations are alien to it, since it gives a comprehensive understanding, on the basis of the Laws of Creation, of the world and of life—beyond nationalities, races, and creeds."*

*Concerning* In the Light of Truth: The Grail Message, *Abd-ru-shin writes:*

> "I wish to fill the gaps which so far have remained unanswered in the souls of men as burning questions, and which never leave any serious thinker in peace."

*Throughout* The Grail Message *readers are urged to weigh questions and answers intuitively, to confront them within their own life experiences, and only to believe that which they can perceive inwardly. Only through this process can one reach true conviction in one's life.*

*What follows is an abstract introducing some of the many principles contained in* The Grail Message. *Full explanations are given within the work itself, and the brief discussion below can in no way substitute for the original.*

49

In the Light of Truth: The Grail Message *explains that human spirits emanated from the spiritual domain at the summit of Creation. God created the universe, and man is a part of that Creation. As such, God stands above Creation and man's place is within Creation. Creation has many different visible and invisible spheres of activity and substance. The meaning of human life on Earth and in the beyond is to develop spiritually so as to return to our primordial origin as fully conscious spirits.*

*When a spirit comes to the material world for the first time in order to mature, it begins to make conscious choices for itself. Choices that do not swing with God's Laws burden the spirit with responsibility to redeem these choices either in the present lifetime, or in the spirit's subsequent reincarnations. Reincarnations provide spirits with direct opportunities to redeem the obligations they have created and to develop towards maturity.*

*God's Laws govern all of Creation, and, since human beings stand within Creation, these laws operate upon them whether or not they acknowledge this fact. Everything in Creation, without exception, is interconnected. Every circumstance in life is a result of the choices a spirit makes, and every circumstance is an opportunity to mature.*

*The Law of Motion: only with motion (vibrations) can there be life, and only with continual striving for ennoblement can there be ascent toward spiritual maturity. The higher one ascends, the faster and lighter are one's vibrations. The lower one descends, the slower and heavier are one's vibrations.*

*The Law of Gravity: everything that is noble, beautiful, pure or light produces an uplifting effect, while everything base, ignoble, or impure produces a sinking, dragging down effect. Therefore, after leaving this earth, every human being will enter that sphere that accords with its density. The Law of Gravity, combined with the Law of Attraction of Homogeneous Species, compels those of similar nature to be together.*

*The Law of Attraction of Homogeneous Species: like attracts like. Whatever emanates from a soul produces vibrations that take on forms corresponding exactly with their nature. Like forms attract each other, creating power centers that affect human beings according to their nature. When combined with the Law of Reciprocal Action, a single thought or action sent out returns strengthened by the Law of Attraction of Homogeneous Species.*

*The Law of Reciprocal Action: individuals reap what they sow; whatever emanates returns. Therefore, we are responsible for our every action and thought. If the action or thought is positive, then we ennoble Creation, and contribute to the advancement of the human race. If our actions or thoughts are negative, they bind us to whoever and whatever we harm, creating a karma that must be redeemed.*

*Individuals have free will. Each can decide whether or not to swing with the Laws in Creation, but the effects react upon them in either case. Human beings stand within Creation, and are responsible for their free choices. Man can only progress through an understanding of and adherence to these Laws.*

*Man's greatest error has been to place himself above God's Will. This arrogance has caused people to go forth blindly with destructive behavior, with thoughts and actions contrary to God's Will, thereby retarding their development toward spiritual maturity. The tool that human beings have most often misused is their intellect. They have overdeveloped the intellect at the cost of their intuition, their true spiritual connection. Indolence of spirit is a great weakness for many people, and the root cause of many of life's problems. This indolence has, over time, caused humans' spiritual abilities to become stunted through lack of use and has allowed the emergence of "intellectual mankind."*

*Within Creation, a multitude of helpers is available to us. Through the Laws of Creation, if an individual emanates pure thoughts and actions, they return strengthened and uplifted by similar thoughts and actions. We attract homogeneous species even more quickly and strongly from the unseen world. Everyone has guides, but most people have cut themselves off from these helps through the overdevelopment of their intellect and negligence of their intuition. Humans must learn to live harmoniously with each other and within Creation: this includes the world of nature.*

*Everything in Creation works in cycles (the Law of Motion). According to their nature, all cycles must end where they began. Human beings do not have unlimited opportunities for reincarnation in order to redeem karma and ascend spiritually. Only by swinging fully with God's Laws will we be able to continue our existence within Creation.*

*God's Justice, as seen in His constant, unvarying Laws, and His creation of humans in the first place, allowing us to live joyously in Creation and to ennoble that which is around us, gives evidence of His great Love.*

In the Light of Truth: The Grail Message *is directed solely to the individual human being, irrespective of creed, nationality or race. It gives comprehensive explanations of the laws that govern the universe including the visible, material world and the various spheres through which the human spirit journeys on its return to its primordial origin. A work which will bring disquiet into many circles, its tone is uplifting, but severe. It requires that each individual is fully responsible for every action and thought produced, whether one accepts that responsibility or not.*

*Other Titles from Grail Foundation Press*

## IN THE LIGHT OF TRUTH: THE GRAIL MESSAGE
•
## THE TEN COMMANDMENTS OF GOD
## THE LORD'S PRAYER
•
## LAO-TSE
•
## BUDDHA
•
## WHY WE LIVE AFTER DEATH

*available at your local bookstore*
*or directly through the publisher*

GRAIL
FOUNDATION PRESS
14318 Shirley Bohn Rd.
Mt. Airy, MD 21771
1-800-427-9217

*Publisher's catalog available on request*

❧

# IN THE LIGHT OF TRUTH: THE GRAIL MESSAGE
## *by Abd-ru-shin*

*In the Light of Truth: The Grail Message* is a classic work that offers clear and perceptive answers to questions which challenge every human being. This collection of 168 essays addresses all spheres of life ranging from God and the Universe to the Laws in Creation, the meaning of life, responsibility, free will, intuition and the intellect, the ethereal world and the beyond, justice and love. *The Grail Message* will appeal to any human being who is seeking to understand life, his or her place in Creation, and the source of one's being.

*Linen edition, three volumes combined*
*ISBN 1-57461-006-6*
*5.5" x 8.5"*
*1,062 pages*
*Paper edition, three-volume boxed set*
*ISBN 1-57461-003-1*
*6" x 9"*
*1,079 pages*

*Original edition: German*
*Translations available in:*
*Czech, Dutch, English, Estonian, French, Hungarian,*
*Italian, Portuguese, Rumanian, Russian,*
*Slovak, Spanish*

# THE TEN COMMANDMENTS OF GOD
# THE LORD'S PRAYER
*by Abd-ru-shin*

Clearly explained in the full, life-embracing meaning, *The Ten Commandments of God and The Lord's Prayer* is a book for anyone striving to live with integrity. Readers who bring these Commandments to life within themselves will find they create a solid foundation for their daily lives and for their existence beyond physical death. Abd-ru-shin's insights regarding the Lord's Prayer help the reader understand this "key to the Kingdom of God" in its profound significance for mankind.

*Linen edition*
*ISBN 1-57461-007-4*
*5" x 7.5"*
*72 pages*
*Paper edition*
*ISBN 1-57461-004-X*
*5" x 7.5"*
*72 pages*

*Original edition: German*
*Translations available in:*
*Czech, Dutch, English, French, Italian, Portuguese,*
*Russian, Slovak, Spanish*

# LAO-TSE
### *The Life and Work*
### *of the Forerunner in China*

Little is known about the life and work of this enlightened Chinese sage. In *Lao-Tse*, the personality of this leader and the events of his life are simply and clearly portrayed. The first in a series, this wonderful story was transcribed from the direct experience of living pictures taken from the Book of Life by one gifted to do so.

*Paper edition*
*ISBN 1-57461-008-2*
*6" x 9"*
*288 Pages*

*Original Edition: German*
*Translations available in:*
*Czech, English, French*

## BUDDHA
### The Life and Work
### of the Forerunner in India

With beauty and grace, this book creates the images of the life of Buddha so that when reading it, one experiences his life as if in living pictures. The story unfolds naturally and is easy and compelling to read. Buddha's relationship to God is clearly defined, and it reveals both the events of his outward life and his inner spiritual development.

The reader sees how Buddha was helped by the events of his life, many of which seemed on the surface to be great misfortune. However, it was through overcoming suffering that Buddha came to the recognition of his purpose in life. His misfortune turned into his greatest help. As a sage of the Word of Truth, he worked in the midst of his people, whom he wished to lead away from a life that submitted indolently to fate to one activated by conviction.

*Paper edition*
*ISBN 1-57461-010-4*
*6" x 9"*
*278 Pages*

*Original Edition: German*
*Translations available in:*
*Czech, English, French*

❧

...........................................................................

## WHY WE LIVE AFTER DEATH
*by Dr. Richard Steinpach*

Accounts of people who had clinically "died" and then been brought back to life are no longer considered fantasy: they have been scientifically proven. However, most writings about life after death have simply reported such accounts and supplied statistical data. Richard Steinpach's work goes much further: by applying Laws of Creation, he explains how we continue to develop after physical death. *Why We Live After Death* opens the door to a fuller understanding of the totality of ur exis-tence, and makes it possible for readers to answer the eternal question, "What is the meaning of life?"

*Paper edition*
*ISBN 1-57461-005-8*
*6" x 9"*
*96 Pages*

*Original Edition: German*
*Translations available in:*
*Czech, Dutch, English, French, Hungarian, Italian,*
*Portuguese, Roumanian, Russian, Slovak, Spanish*

*over 500,000 copies printed*

...........................................................................